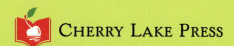

Published in the United States of America by Cherry Lake Publishing Group
Ann Arbor, Michigan
www.cherrylakepublishing.com

Reading Adviser: Beth Walker Gambro, MS, Ed., Reading Consultant, Yorkville, IL

Photo Credits: © PrathanChorruangsak/iStockPhoto, cover; © Gorodenkoff/Shutterstock, 5; © Mergeldea/Shutterstock, 7; © DC Studio/Shutterstock, 8; © 22Images Studio/Shutterstock, 9; © DC Studio/Shutterstock, 11; © Tada Images/Shutterstock, 12; © Monkey Business Images/Shutterstock, 13; © Stock-Asso/Shutterstock, 14; © Alex Photo Stock/Shutterstock, 15; © DC Studio/Shutterstock, 17; © Stas Knop/Shutterstock, 18; © Frame Stock Footage/Shutterstock; © Igisheva Maria/Shutterstock, 21; © Andrey_Popov/Shutterstock, 22; © Yaroslav Astakhov/Shutterstock, 23; © SeventyFour/Shutterstock, 24; © PeopleImages.com - Yuri A/Shutterstock, 25; © Tutatamafilm/Shutterstock, 27; © Gorodenkoff/Shutterstock, 28; © doublelee/Shutterstock, 29; © Frame Stock Footage/Shutterstock, 31

Copyright © 2026 by Cherry Lake Publishing Group
All rights reserved. No part of this book may be reproduced or utilized in any form or by any means without written permission from the publisher.

Cherry Lake Press is an imprint of Cherry Lake Publishing Group.

Library of Congress Cataloging-in-Publication Data has been filed and is available at catalog.loc.gov.

Cherry Lake Publishing Group would like to acknowledge the work of the Partnership for 21st Century Learning, a Network of Battelle for Kids. Please visit Battelle for Kids online for more information.

Printed in the United States of America

Note from publisher: Websites change regularly, and their future contents are outside of our control. Supervise children when conducting any recommended online searches for extended learning opportunities.

Diane Lindsey Reeves likes to write books that help students figure out what they want to be when they grow up. She mostly lives in Washington, D.C., but spends as much time as she can in North Carolina and South Carolina with her grandkids.

CONTENTS

Introduction:

In the Know | 4

Chapter 1:

**Video Game Designers Know...
How to Play the Game | 6**

Chapter 2:

**Video Game Designers Know...
All About Video Games | 10**

Chapter 3:

**Video Game Designers Know...
The Tools of the Trade | 16**

Chapter 4:

**Video Game Designers Know...
How to Work Safely | 20**

Chapter 5:

**Video Game Designers Know...
How to Find the Job They Want | 26**

Stop, Think, and Write | 30

Things to Do If You Want to Be a Video Game Designer | 30

Learn More | 31

Glossary, Index | 32

In the Know

Every career you can imagine has one thing in common: It takes an expert. Career experts need to know more about how to do a specific job than other people do. That's how everyone from plumbers to rocket scientists gets their job done.

Sometimes it takes years of college study to learn what they need to know. Other times, people learn by working alongside someone who is already a career expert. No matter how they learn, it takes a career expert to do any job well.

Take video game designers, for instance. They get paid to make games that people love to play! It's a gamer's dream come true. Even so, it takes amazing technical and creative skills to make those games happen. Video game designers are at the top of their game (pun intended!) when it comes to creating imaginary worlds that gamers can't stop visiting.

Is a career designing video games in your future? Keep reading to find out more.

Video game designers are good at:

- Brainstorming new game ideas
- Juggling several different roles
- Creating visual content for games
- Using software to program computer code
- Working as part of a team

CHAPTER 1

Video Game Designers Know...How to Play the Game

Video gaming is a global obsession. There are 3.2 billion video gamers in the world, and 1.17 billion play games online. People play to relieve stress and relax. They play to connect with friends and have fun. Some even play to learn.

With more than 5 million video games to choose from, there is a game for everyone to enjoy. Some video games are just for play. Others provide fun learning experiences. Popular video games include *Minecraft*, *Fortnite*, *Super Mario Brothers*, *Candy Crush*, and *Angry Birds*. *Oregon Trail*, *Math Blaster*, and the *Magic School Bus* are examples of fun learning games.

Gamers use headsets and sound systems to connect with friends over long distances. They talk to one another while playing.

Skilled video game designers use complex software to create games. They learn in school and on the job how to master this software.

Video game designers are the professionals who keep the games coming. Video games are a mix of computer science, computer programming, graphic design, user experience, and creative writing. Game designers need skills and experience that bring all of these areas together.

Some video game designers have college degrees in computer science, computer programming, or video game design. Other game designers master these skills through a variety of online learning experiences and boot camps. These types of programs concentrate on the skills a person needs to create games. Although a college degree isn't always required, it can help land top jobs.

Video game designers know that technical skills are a must for success in this career. They also know that the best game designers are very creative. Good ideas make the difference between good video games and great ones.

VIDEO GAME FIRSTS

Physicist William Higinbotham is said to have invented the first video game in 1958. It was called *Tennis for Two*. It was the first **analog** computer game.

Speaking of firsts, *Tetris* by Nintendo was the first video game played in space. Russian cosmonaut Aleksandr Serebrov played it aboard the Mir space station in 1993.

CHAPTER 2

Video Game Designers Know...All About Video Games

One thing that most video game designers share is a love of video games. It is likely that they've been playing games since they were kids like you. These experiences provided a first lesson in what video games are all about.

Playing video games is one of the best ways to learn about different kinds of gameplay. Action-adventure games are the most popular type of video games. This includes all the fighting, racing, and shooting games that pit one player against another. In role-playing games (RPGs), the player controls the action of a character in a well-defined world. Simulation games like *SimCity* put players in situations where they solve real-world problems. Sandbox games involve world-building tasks.

Action adventure games provide a sense of competition. Experienced players want to win.

2048 is a popular sliding tile puzzle game created by Italian video game designer Gabriele Cirulli.

There are also word games, puzzle games, and more. They all make for exciting opportunities to create new player experiences. What is your favorite type of game?

Video game designers know that all types of video games share common ingredients. They all work on a core **gameplay loop**. Players engage with repeatable actions throughout a game that create a fun experience. These fun experiences keep players coming back. Often, these loops build in complexity and allow successful players to play at higher levels.

Dedicated gamers often have a large desk with multiple screens. They buy the best software for the best experience.

Video game designers create good stories for both single and multiplayer games. Some stories are more fun to play through with friends!

Video game designers know that many good games are built around good stories. Many characters and the game's world emerge as the story unfolds. Stories may be linear and take players from beginning to end. Or they may branch off in different directions depending on the actions of the players. Either way, a good game story, like a good book, keeps players wanting to play more.

Strong characters keep players engaged. Appealing design creates game worlds that players want to visit.

Keeping players coming back for more is how video games become bestsellers. Video game designers know that keeping players motivated is key to the game's success. Players get hooked on rewards and challenges. They enjoy competing with themselves and others to get to the next level.

BEST OF THE BEST

Minecraft by Mojang is the bestselling video game of all time. It was released in 2011 and has sold more than 300 million copies. As of 2024, there were more than 204 million monthly players still playing it. Some describe the game as "online LEGO®." Players use building blocks to create structures in different environments and terrains. *Minecraft*'s virtual world involves players in resource gathering, building, and combat.

CHAPTER 3

Video Game Designers Know...The Tools of the Trade

Video game designers know that, before the fun begins, there is plenty of work to do. Video games are like gigantic puzzles. Designers make sure that all the pieces fall into place.

Project manager is one of the many roles a game designer may play. Project managers use special software to keep track of tasks, deadlines, and teammates. These tools let project teams communicate with each other. They share files and videos. They come together for virtual meetings.

All video games start with an idea. The first idea sparks more ideas. Before you know it, there are ideas floating around everywhere. Video game designers may use a mind-mapping tool to organize ideas. This tool helps them separate the good ideas from the duds. It is a visual tool that lets them see how gameplay might work.

Like many professions, being a good video game designer means knowing how to work with a team. Bouncing problems and ideas off of teammates is critical.

Video games are built around stories. Video game designers use **storyboarding** software to plot how images, sound, and action come together. Storyboards help designers chart each step of the game with separate columns for each element. This process is similar to making a movie.

What would a video game be without a cast of characters? Video game designers work with various artists who use a variety of 2-dimensional (2D) and 3-dimensional (3D) animation tools.

HOW DOES IT RATE?

There are so many video games on the market now. It can be tricky to figure out which ones are for kids and which ones are for adults. That's why the Entertainment Software Rating Board (ESRB) came up with a rating system. People use these ratings to make good choices about games.

The system uses letters to identify a game's intended audience. *E* stands for everyone. These games are fun and safe for all ages to play. *E10+* is a little more complicated. They are best for kids ages 10 and older. *T* stands for teens. *M* is for more mature audiences who are at least 17 years old. An *A* rating means the game is for adults only. These games are best used by people who are at least 18 years old.

Video games go through many trial runs before hitting the shelves. Often, the design process takes up to 5 years!

Prototypes are a big tool in game development. That's when the game designer puts all the different pieces together for a test run. A prototype is like a rough draft of the game. It lets testers find out if the game is fun and works as it is intended. This step helps game designers identify problems and make changes before the actual game is produced.

All the different pieces finally come together with game engine technology. This tool is where the actual game is developed. It is home base for all the different parts of the game.

CHAPTER 4

Video Game Designers Know...How to Work Safely

Video game designers don't face the same risks as other professions, like skilled trades. They don't have to worry about falling off a ladder or cutting themselves with a saw. They use software, not the hardware you find in a toolbox. Even so, they do need to take care of some physical safety concerns.

Like other professionals who work on computers all day, game designers are at risk of physical injuries. The most common injury is carpal tunnel syndrome. This is a painful condition that affects hands and wrists. It is caused by the repetitive movement of typing on a keyboard. It is treated with rest, ice, and splints. Severe problems may require surgery to repair pinched nerves.

To avoid carpal tunnel, practice good posture and take breaks between typing tasks.

Try to find an office chair that supports your lower back. This helps avoid strain on your muscles.

Back and neck pain are common complaints for video game designers. Eye strain can be an issue, too. These problems are caused by sitting in a chair and staring at a screen for long periods of time.

The good news is that there are ways to prevent these kinds of physical injuries. Taking frequent stretch breaks is a simple solution. A big solution is **ergonomics**. Ergonomics is the science of fitting a workplace to the worker's needs.

Ergonomic engineers look for ways to keep workers more comfortable and productive at work. Ergonomic chairs and keyboards help prevent injuries. The quality and design of computer screens help reduce eye strain and relieve physical fatigue.

VIDEO GAMES GO PRO

What's the next best thing to playing video games yourself? It's watching professional video gamers compete for money and fame. Electronic sports, or **esports**, are exploding in popularity. Even schools and universities are joining in to compete.

Educators like esports because competitive gaming can benefit students. It encourages collaboration, creativity, and inclusion. It builds important skills such as problem-solving, teamwork, and communication.

Another key benefit is that esports let students experience STEM (science, technology, engineering, and math) in action. In the process, they are exposed to all kinds of career options. This includes everything from video and sound editing to graphic design, broadcasting, and event planning. Who knew that playing video games could be so good for you?

Esports tournaments can be up to a week long, depending on the number of teams and the length of the games.

A key way to avoid burnout is to manage your workload well. Excellent time management is key.

Video game designers also deal with mental health issues. Their work requires a lot of brain power. Keeping creative ideas coming and juggling all of their tasks can be stressful. Sometimes video game designers experience **burnout**. This is best described as someone running out of steam. Rest and relaxation are often the best cures.

CHAPTER 5

Video Game Designers Know...How to Find the Job They Want

Video game designers aren't the only players when it comes to creating video games. They are certainly in the middle of all the action. But other professionals add their talent and skills to make video games successful. Some help make the games. Others help sell the finished product.

Animators are super talented graphic designers who create the characters, backgrounds, and action scenes used in a game. They often start with notebook sketches and use computers to create both 2D and 3D images of the game's virtual world.

Artificial intelligence (AI) programmers give the game its brain. They create **algorithms** that define each character's behaviors and actions.

Some of your favorite video game characters, like Mario or Pikachu, started as nothing more than a notebook sketch!

Gameplay programmers handle the technical side of the process. They write the computer code that makes the game work.

Game testers are like video game spies. As they play the games, they are on the lookout for problems. Does everything work as it is supposed to? Does play get bogged down or even boring at certain points? It's their job to investigate!

Sound designers integrate the music, voices, and background noises that bring a game to life. Also called audio engineers, they use microphones, computers, mixing boards, and other audio equipment to do their jobs.

HELP WANTED

Video games bring in billions of dollars in revenue. It is a big industry that is expected to continue to grow. But, the games aren't the only competitive part of the business. The best jobs go to the most talented video game designers.

Stores that sell video games prepare in advance for game releases. Then they make sure to keep the most popular games stocked.

Publishers own the companies that make video games. They put the games up for sale online and in stores. Publishing teams take care of everything from funding the project to building game websites.

Marketing teams use publicity, advertising, and other ways to sell the product. Their job is to get the word out and build demand for the game. Bestseller list, watch out!

Esports is a growing industry where video game players compete, often in front of live audiences or on live broadcasts. Esport teams and events bring new career opportunities. Esport managers organize events. Esport coaches manage teams.

Activity

Stop, Think, and Write

Can you imagine a world without video game designers? How do they make the places we live, work, and play better?

Get a separate sheet of paper. On one side, answer this question:

- *How do video game designers make the world a better place?*

On the other side of the paper:

- *Draw a picture of you standing next to characters from your bestselling video game.*

Things to Do If You Want to Be a Video Game Designer

Want to be a video game designer? Only the best candidates get chosen for the job. But don't worry! You can start preparing now! It all starts with a love of video games. From there, it takes training and experience.

NOW

- Play video games.
- Learn computer programming languages like Python.
- Take computer animation classes in school.
- Look into esport opportunities at your school or in your community.
- Start building simple games now on platforms like Scratch, Roblox, or GameMaker.

LATER

- Consider earning a college degree in computer science, computer programming, or video game design.
- Look into online programs and boot camps that focus on specific game design skills.
- Build a portfolio showing examples of your best work.
- Get experience working as an intern in a video game or software development company.

Learn More

Books

Rathburn, Betsy. *Video Game Developer.* Minneapolis, MN: Bellwether Media, 2023.

Steel, Craig. *Ultimate Gamer Career Mode: The Complete Guide to Starting a Career in Gaming.* New York, NY: Kingfisher, 2021.

Wessels, Marcie. *The Boy Who Thought Outside the Box: The Story of Game Designer Ralph Baer.* New York, NY: Sterling Children's Books, 2020.

On the Web

With an adult, learn more online with these suggested searches.

Inspire My Kids — Careers that Count: So You Want to Be a Video Game Designer?

Massachusetts Institute of Technology (MIT) — Scratch

PBS Learning Media — Careers in Video Game Development — Video

31

Glossary

algorithms (AL-guh-rih-thuhmz) processes or sets of rules to be followed in calculations or problem-solving operations

analog (AA-nuh-log) technology that uses moving parts to show a continuous change in information

artificial intelligence (ar-tuh-FIH-shuhl in-TEH-luh-juhns) computers and machines that run complex code to duplicate and predict human tasks and language

burnout (BUHRN-owt) physical and emotional exhaustion caused by prolonged stress

ergonomics (er-guh-NAH-miks) science concerned with designing and maintaining efficient and safe work equipment and environments

esports (EE-sports) public video game competitions in which professional gamers compete

gameplay loop (GAYM-play LOOP) series of repeatable actions throughout a video game

prototypes (PROH-tuh-tieps) first versions of a product

storyboarding (STOR-ee-bohr-ding) process of visualizing a video game or movie sequence into individual panels

Index

activities, 30
art and animation, 18, 26–27
artificial intelligence (AI), 26

back and neck pain, 22
burnout, 25

carpal tunnel syndrome, 20–21
creative skills, 4–5, 8–9, 16, 18, 26–27

education, 4, 8–9, 30
Entertainment Software Rating Board, 18
ergonomics, 20–23
esports, 23–24, 29–30
eye strain, 22–23

game engine technology, 19
gameplay, 10, 12, 14–15, 28
game testers, 19, 28

job market, 28, 30

marketing, 29
Minecraft (game), 15

project managers, 16
prototypes, 19, 28
publishers, 29

ratings systems, 18
repetitive stress injuries, 20–23

safety, 20–23, 25
sales, 28–29
software, 5, 8, 16, 18
sound designers, 28
stories and storyboarding, 14, 18
study and training, 4, 8–9, 30

teamwork
designers, 5, 16–17, 19
players, 7, 14

technical skills, 4–5, 8–9, 16, 19, 28, 30
Tennis for Two (game), 9
testing, 19, 28
Tetris (game), 9
time management, 25
2048 (game), 12

video game designers
job descriptions, 8, 12, 14–19, 26–29
skills, 4–5, 8–9, 16, 18–19, 26–28, 30
tools, 8, 16–19, 26
video games
accessories, 7, 13
competitive, 23–24, 29–30
players, 6–7, 10–13, 23–24, 29
ratings, 18
types and titles, 6, 9–12, 14–15, 18, 29

32